1 MIND-BLOWING WAR STORIES

100 Unbelievable Tales of Bravery, Strategy, and Survival

FELIX GRAYSON

MINDSPARK
PUBLISHING

CONTENTS

BEFORE WE DIVE IN...

Did you know that this is just **one** of many **mind-blowing** books waiting to be discovered?

What if I told you there's a **world of jaw-dropping, unbelievable, and downright bizarre facts** across **sports, science, history, mysteries, and more**—each one packed with stories that will **challenge what you thought you knew?**

EVER WONDERED WHAT IT'S LIKE TO...

- Witness **record-breaking Olympic moments** that defy human limits?

- Explore **real-life conspiracy theories** that sound too wild to be true?

- Discover **unsolved mysteries** that still leave experts baffled?

- Learn about **billionaires, stock market**

crashes, and money secrets?

- Find out how **robots, AI, and space travel are shaping the future?**

- Experience the **most extreme sports, legendary battles, and shocking events?**

This is just the beginning. The **100 Mind-Blowing series** covers it **all.**

WANT TO SEE WHAT'S NEXT?

Go to **FelixGrayson.com** and explore the **growing collection** of books and audiobooks that will **entertain, amaze, and keep you coming back for more.**

Curiosity doesn't stop here—this is just the beginning. What will blow your mind next?

INTRODUCTION

Welcome to *100 Mind-Blowing War Stories*, a collection designed to make you say, "No way that actually happened." From unbelievable heroics to bizarre battlefield twists, this book dives deep into the strange, wild, and often jaw-dropping moments that history class somehow forgot to mention.

Ever heard of the time a pigeon stopped an airstrike? Or when a pirate queen outmaneuvered entire empires? What about the soldier who mailed himself to freedom—or the general who forgot his army? These stories—and 96 more like them—are waiting for you inside. Each one has been carefully selected to surprise, entertain, and remind us that in war, truth is often stranger than fiction.

Whether you're a history buff, a trivia lover, or just someone who enjoys a great story, this book offers something unexpected on every page. Read it straight through, or flip to a random entry whenever you're in the mood for a dose of the unbelievable. There's no wrong way to explore this wild ride through the past.

So get comfortable, maybe brew some coffee (or dig a trench?), and prepare for an unforgettable journey through the most outrageous, inspiring, and mind-blowing moments in the history of warfare. Let's begin.

Mind-Blowing War Story #1

THE SOLDIER WHO SAVED D-DAY

During the Normandy invasion, a lost paratrooper may have changed the course of history—with a bag of bugles.

Private John Steele of the 82nd Airborne was one of thousands dropped behind enemy lines in the early hours of D-Day. But his parachute snagged on the church steeple in Sainte-Mère-Église, leaving him dangling helplessly above the square during a fierce firefight. He played dead for hours as German troops moved below him, eventually being taken prisoner—only to escape and rejoin his unit days later. The delay caused by the battle in the town, sparked partly by Steele's unexpected appearance, helped Allied forces secure a key route inland. Today, a parachute effigy still hangs from that same steeple in his honor.

Mind-Blowing War Story #2

THE GHOST ARMY THAT FOOLED HITLER

The Allies created an entire fake army—and the Nazis fell for it.

During World War II, the U.S. military deployed the 23rd Headquarters Special Troops, better known as the "Ghost Army." Their mission? Trick the Germans using inflatable tanks, fake radio transmissions, and sound effects blasted from massive speakers. These master deceivers staged more than 20 battlefield illusions across Europe, convincing enemy forces that major Allied units were in places they weren't. In one operation, they faked an entire division—complete with tire tracks, fake generals, and phony chatter—helping divert German attention away from real troop movements. Their top-secret efforts weren't declassified until the 1990s.

Mind-Blowing War Story #3

THE PILOT WHO CHASED A BOMBER ON FOOT

When his bomber took off without him, he sprinted after it—and caught it.

During World War II, U.S. pilot James Howell was preparing for takeoff in his B-17 Flying Fortress when the brakes failed and the plane began rolling down the runway—without him. With no one at the controls and the engines roaring, the massive bomber was gaining speed. In a moment of pure adrenaline and desperation, Howell *ran after the plane*, climbed aboard through an open hatch, and managed to stop it before it crashed into anything. His quick thinking not only saved the aircraft but also the lives of everyone on the airfield. To this day, it remains one of the most bizarre aircraft "takeoffs" in military history.

Mind-Blowing War Story #4

THE SPY WHO WROTE IN INVISIBLE URINE

A British spy used his own pee to send secret messages.

During World War I, British intelligence officer Mansfield Cumming—yes, that was his real name—discovered that urine could be used as invisible ink. His agents were instructed to "write between the lines" with their bodily fluid, which would later be revealed by heating the paper. The method was surprisingly effective until it started… to smell. Eventually, the intelligence service switched to chemical alternatives, but for a time, this bizarre technique was a legitimate espionage tool. Cumming is also credited with founding what would become MI6, and his experiments in secret communication laid the groundwork for future spycraft.

Mind-Blowing War Story #5

THE SAMURAI WHO FOUGHT IN WORLD WAR II

He charged into battle with a sword—and survived.

Takeo Sasaki, a Japanese officer during World War II, brought ancient tradition into modern warfare—by wielding a samurai sword on the battlefield. While most soldiers carried rifles, Sasaki charged into enemy lines during the Battle of Saipan *with a katana*. Witnesses claimed he cut down multiple American troops in close combat before being wounded and captured. His actions weren't just symbolic; Japanese officers often carried swords as both weapons and emblems of honor. Though rare, there were several accounts of sword-wielding charges during the war, but Sasaki's is one of the few where the samurai survived—and lived to tell the tale.

Mind-Blowing War Story #6

THE POW CAMP THAT FOOLED THE NAZIS

Allied prisoners built a fake war camp—inside a real one.

In Stalag Luft III, a German POW camp during World War II, Allied airmen orchestrated one of the most daring escapes in history—by constructing a fake escape operation to *distract from the real one*. While guards watched a decoy tunnel and monitored suspicious activities above ground, the prisoners were secretly digging **three** full-length tunnels named Tom, Dick, and Harry. Their decoys included fake uniforms, forged documents, and even *a wooden vaulting horse* used to hide dirt disposal. On the night of March 24, 1944, 76 men escaped through Tunnel Harry. While most were recaptured, the sheer brilliance of the plan shook the Nazis—and later inspired the film *The Great Escape*.

Mind-Blowing War Story #7

THE GENERAL WHO PLAYED DEAD

He survived a massacre by pretending to be a corpse.

During the brutal Katyn Massacre of 1940, Soviet forces executed over 20,000 Polish officers, hoping to wipe out the country's military leadership. One man, General Władysław Anders, miraculously escaped the slaughter—not by fighting, but by *playing dead*. After being shot and dumped into a mass grave, Anders regained consciousness and lay perfectly still among the bodies until nightfall. Covered in blood and dirt, he crawled from the pit and fled to safety. Against all odds, he later commanded Polish forces alongside the Allies and became a national hero. His survival became a symbol of resilience in the face of unspeakable horror.

Mind-Blowing War Story #8

THE NURSE WHO RESCUED A NAZI GENERAL

She saved the enemy—and changed the war's course.

In 1943, British nurse Jean Rennie was treating wounded soldiers in North Africa when she discovered one of her patients was no ordinary German—he was **General Wilhelm Ritter von Thoma**, a high-ranking officer captured during the Second Battle of El Alamein. Rennie's expert care helped nurse him back to health, and during his recovery, von Thoma let slip key details about Hitler's prized V-2 rocket program—details British intelligence had been desperately seeking. His accidental confession, overheard by MI6 through hidden microphones, helped accelerate Allied efforts to sabotage the program before it could wreak havoc across Europe.

Mind-Blowing War Story #9

THE SOLDIER WHO CAPTURED 132 ALONE

One man. One machine gun. Total chaos for the enemy.

In 1918, during World War I's Meuse-Argonne Offensive, U.S. soldier **Alvin C. York** found himself and a handful of men ambushed behind German lines. With most of his unit pinned down or killed, York charged forward alone, taking out a machine gun nest with precise rifle fire and his Colt .45. He continued to advance, shooting and capturing stunned German troops as he went—eventually rounding up **132 prisoners** *by himself*. His solo assault was so unbelievable that military officials initially didn't believe the reports. York was later awarded the Medal of Honor and became one of the most celebrated American war heroes of all time.

Mind-Blowing War Story #10

THE PIGEON THAT SAVED A BATTALION

A bird flew through gunfire to stop a bombing.

During World War I, a carrier pigeon named **Cher Ami** delivered a message that saved nearly 200 American soldiers. The "Lost Battalion" had been trapped behind enemy lines and was being bombed by their own artillery, who thought they were German troops. With their last hope resting on a pigeon, the men released Cher Ami—who was immediately shot through the breast, blinded in one eye, and had a leg hanging by a tendon. *But she kept flying.* Against all odds, she delivered the message to headquarters in time to stop the shelling. She was awarded the French Croix de Guerre and stuffed for display—hero status, fully earned.

Mind-Blowing War Story #11

THE SUB THAT SANK A TRAIN

A German U-boat took out a train. From the ocean.

In 1918, the German submarine **U-156** pulled off one of the strangest attacks in World War I history. After surfacing off the coast of Orleans, Massachusetts—the only World War I attack on U.S. soil—the crew opened fire with deck guns on a nearby shipyard and surrounding area. As shells rained down, a passing train carrying military supplies happened to be in the line of fire. The U-boat's shells hit the train, derailing it and causing chaos inland—all while still floating offshore. Though the damage was limited, it was a shocking reminder that even trains weren't safe from the sea.

Mind-Blowing War Story #12

THE WAR THAT WAS OVER IN 38 MINUTES

History's shortest war barely got started.

In 1896, the Anglo-Zanzibar War broke out between the British Empire and the Sultanate of Zanzibar—and it ended **38 minutes later**. After the Sultan refused to step down following the death of a British-backed ruler, the Royal Navy opened fire on the palace. The Sultan's forces were quickly overwhelmed: his palace was destroyed, his artillery silenced, and his yacht sunk in the harbor. By the time the smoke cleared, the Sultan had fled, and a British-approved successor took power. It was technically a war—but it barely lasted long enough for breakfast.

Mind-Blowing War Story #13

THE WOMAN WHO BECAME A PIRATE QUEEN

She led a navy against the British Empire—and won.

In the early 1800s, **Ching Shih**, a former Cantonese prostitute turned pirate, commanded one of the largest pirate fleets in history—over 300 ships and 40,000 men. When the Qing Dynasty, Portuguese Navy, and British Empire *all* tried to stop her, she defeated them **repeatedly** in open sea battles. Her naval dominance forced the Chinese government to offer her amnesty... with full rights, wealth, and even the freedom to keep her loot. She retired peacefully, ran a gambling house, and died of old age—a fate nearly unheard of for pirates, let alone pirate queens.

Mind-Blowing War Story #14

THE SOLDIER WHO ESCAPED BY ROWBOAT

He crossed the North Sea alone—in a rowboat.

In 1941, Norwegian resistance fighter **Jan Baalsrud** was the sole survivor of a Nazi ambush during a covert operation. Wounded, frostbitten, and hunted across the Arctic, he trekked through snow-covered mountains, dug himself into a cave to hide from search parties, and even *amputated his own frostbitten toes* with a pocketknife. But the wildest part? He escaped to Sweden by rowing a small boat **over 80 miles across the icy North Sea**—completely alone. He survived, returned to fight, and later became a national hero in Norway. His journey remains one of the most harrowing survival stories of World War II.

Mind-Blowing War Story #15

THE WAR THAT STARTED OVER A BUCKET

Yes, a wooden bucket triggered a full-blown war.

In 1325, tensions between the Italian city-states of Modena and Bologna exploded after Modenese soldiers **stole a wooden bucket** from a Bologna city well. It wasn't just a prank—it was seen as a national insult. What followed was the **War of the Oaken Bucket**, a bloody conflict involving thousands of troops. Modena defeated Bologna at the Battle of Zappolino and kept the bucket as a trophy. To this day, the infamous bucket is still on display in Modena, proudly showcased as a symbol of one of the strangest causes of war in history.

Mind-Blowing War Story #16

THE BATTLESHIP THAT REFUSED TO SINK

It took 24 hours, 85 bombs, and still it floated.

During the attack on Pearl Harbor in 1941, the **USS Nevada** was the only U.S. battleship to get underway during the assault. Japanese bombers targeted it aggressively, hoping to sink it in the harbor and block the channel. The Nevada was hit with multiple bombs and torpedoes, set ablaze, and still kept moving. Eventually, to avoid sinking in a critical spot, the crew **beached the ship intentionally**. Even after being battered for over a full day, she didn't go down. The Nevada was repaired, returned to service, and later took part in D-Day and the invasion of Okinawa. Some ships are just built different.

Mind-Blowing
War Story #17

THE EXPLODING ANIMAL BOMBS

The Allies tried turning bats into tiny bombers.

In one of World War II's stranger experiments, the U.S. military developed **"bat bombs"**—tiny incendiary devices strapped to real, live bats. The idea was to release them over Japanese cities, where the bats would roost in wooden buildings before the timed explosives detonated, causing widespread fires. Code-named **Project X-Ray**, the plan actually worked in tests—one trial accidentally burned down a U.S. airfield. Despite initial success, the project was scrapped in favor of the atomic bomb. Still, for a brief moment in history, the military genuinely believed bats might win the war.

Mind-Blowing War Story #18

THE ARMY THAT FROZE IN PLACE

An entire invasion force was defeated by weather.

In 1812, Napoleon Bonaparte led over **600,000 troops** into Russia—the largest army Europe had ever seen. But instead of facing defeat in battle, Napoleon's **Grande Armée** was wrecked by **winter**. Russian forces used a scorched earth tactic, retreating while burning villages and supplies. With no food, warmth, or shelter, soldiers froze by the thousands. Temperatures plummeted to -30°C (-22°F), and by the time the army limped back to France, fewer than **100,000 men** remained. The disastrous campaign shattered Napoleon's power and proved that sometimes, the fiercest general is *nature itself.*

Mind-Blowing War Story #19

THE PRESIDENT WHO WENT TO WAR

A sitting U.S. president fought *on the front lines*.

In 1814, during the War of 1812, **President James Madison** became the only sitting U.S. president to **enter an active battlefield**. As British forces advanced on Washington, D.C., Madison personally rode out with American troops to scout the front lines. He even armed himself with a pair of pistols. Though he didn't fire a shot, his presence during the chaotic defense of the capital was real—and risky. Hours later, British troops invaded and **burned the White House**. Madison narrowly escaped, but his battlefield appearance remains one of the most daring—and surreal—moments in presidential history.

Mind-Blowing War Story #20

THE SOLDIER WHO PLAYED DEAD TWICE

He faked his death—then did it again to escape.

British soldier **Eddie Chapman** was a safe-cracker-turned-spy during World War II, and his life played out like a Hollywood script. Captured by the Nazis while imprisoned on Jersey Island, Chapman convinced them he was willing to spy for Germany. After para-chuting into England, he immediately **turned himself in** and became a British double agent. When the Gestapo suspected something, Chapman **faked his own death** to throw them off. It worked—twice. He fed false intel to the Nazis for years, earning their Iron Cross *while secretly working for MI5.* Few spies ever played both sides so effectively—and survived.

Mind-Blowing War Story #21

THE TIME SWITZERLAND ACCIDENTALLY INVADED

They crossed the border... by mistake.

In 2007, a group of **Swiss infantry soldiers** on a night exercise accidentally **invaded Liechtenstein**—a neighboring country with no army. Poor weather and outdated maps led the troops about a mile over the border before anyone realized the error. When the Swiss government apologized, Liechtenstein officials calmly replied they hadn't even noticed. No shots were fired, and the entire "invasion" ended with a chuckle and some diplomatic backpedaling. It remains one of the most polite and harmless military blunders in modern history—and a reminder that even neutral nations can have an off day.

Mind-Blowing War Story #22

THE PIANIST WHO FOOLED THE NAZIS

He survived the Holocaust by playing Chopin.

Polish-Jewish pianist **Władysław Szpilman** was hiding in the ruins of Warsaw during the Nazi occupation when he was discovered by a German officer. But instead of arresting or executing him, the officer **asked him to play the piano** in a deserted house. Szpilman, weak and starving, played a haunting Chopin piece that moved the officer to tears. The German, Captain Wilm Hosenfeld, secretly brought him food and supplies for weeks—saving his life. After the war, Szpilman became a celebrated composer, and his story was later immortalized in the Oscar-winning film *The Pianist*.

Mind-Blowing War Story #23

THE NAVY BLIMP THAT LANDED EMPTY

The crew vanished mid-flight—without a trace.

In 1942, a U.S. Navy blimp called **L-8** took off from Treasure Island in San Francisco Bay on a routine patrol for enemy submarines. Hours later, it drifted back inland and made a soft crash landing in Daly City. But when rescuers arrived, they found something chilling: **the cabin was empty.** Both crewmen had vanished without any signs of struggle, damage, or distress. Parachutes and life vests were untouched. The blimp was intact. Despite an investigation, no definitive explanation was ever found. It remains one of the most eerie unsolved mysteries of World War II.

Mind-Blowing War Story #24

THE DOG THAT BECAME A SERGEANT

He started as a stray—and outranked some soldiers.

In World War I, an abandoned pit bull mix named **Stubby** wandered into a U.S. Army training camp and was adopted by soldiers of the 102nd Infantry. Smuggled aboard a ship to Europe, Stubby became a battlefield legend. He **warned troops of gas attacks**, located wounded soldiers, and even **captured a German spy** by grabbing his pants and holding on until help arrived. His bravery earned him the rank of **Sergeant**, making him the first dog ever promoted through combat. Stubby returned home a hero, met presidents, and marched in parades—proof that not all war heroes walk on two legs.

Mind-Blowing War Story #25

THE CITY THAT SURRENDERED TO A DUMMY

A cardboard tank convinced them to give up.

In World War II, the Allies devised a bold bluff to liberate the French port city of Le Havre. Rather than risk high casualties, they deployed fake **inflatable tanks and artillery**, backed by loudspeakers simulating engine noise and fake radio chatter. The Germans, unaware it was all a ruse, believed a full-scale invasion force was outside their gates—and **surrendered without a fight**. This wasn't the only time deception won a battle, but Le Havre's fall to **rubber tanks and clever sound effects** remains one of the greatest cons in wartime history.

Mind-Blowing War Story #26

THE GENERAL WHO LOST TO EMUS

A ustralia went to war... and the emus won.

In 1932, Australia launched a full-scale military operation to combat an unexpected enemy: **emus**. Thousands of the large, flightless birds were damaging farmland in Western Australia, so soldiers armed with machine guns were sent to eliminate them. But the emus were faster and smarter than expected—they scattered, dodged bullets, and outmaneuvered trucks. After weeks of effort, the soldiers had used **thousands of rounds** and barely made a dent. The operation was quietly called off, and the emus emerged victorious. The so-called **Emu War** remains one of history's most unintentionally hilarious military campaigns.

Mind-Blowing War Story #27

THE PRISON CAMP BUILT FROM MONOPOLY

Secret maps and tools were hidden in board games.

During World War II, the British government partnered with the makers of **Monopoly** to aid prisoners of war held by the Nazis. Special edition Monopoly sets were sent to POW camps through fake humanitarian organizations. But these weren't ordinary games—they contained **silk maps** hidden under the board, **real money** mixed with play cash, and even **tiny compasses and files** tucked inside the pieces. The games helped hundreds of Allied prisoners plan escapes across occupied Europe. It was one of the most clever and successful uses of civilian products for covert operations in the entire war.

Mind-Blowing War Story #28

THE ASSASSIN WITH A CANDY BOX

A bomb disguised as chocolates nearly killed Hitler.

In 1943, British intelligence devised a plot to assassinate Adolf Hitler using an explosive hidden inside a **box of fancy chocolates**. The plan was for a double agent to smuggle the deadly sweets into the German high command's dining area, where Hitler often snacked. The box looked elegant and harmless, but once opened, it would trigger a deadly explosion. The plot was foiled when British officials leaked the plan—fearing the assassination might backfire politically. The "chocolate bomb" is now a bizarre footnote in espionage history—and a chilling reminder that even desserts weren't safe in wartime.

Mind-Blowing War Story #29

THE BATTLE FOUGHT AFTER THE WAR

They didn't know the war was over—and kept fighting.

On December 16, 1945—**more than a month after World War II officially ended**—a Japanese holdout unit on Morotai Island in Indonesia launched a surprise attack on Allied forces. Unaware that Japan had surrendered in August, the soldiers had been hiding in the jungle, cut off from all communication. Believing the war was still raging, they staged a raid on an Allied airfield, wounding several before being captured. This wasn't an isolated case—**some Japanese soldiers held out for decades**, refusing to believe the war had ended. One of them, Hiroo Onoda, didn't surrender until **1974**.

Mind-Blowing War Story #30

THE BLIND MAN WHO SHOT DOWN A PLANE

He couldn't see—but he never missed.

During the Winter War between Finland and the Soviet Union in 1939, Finnish soldier **Aarne Juutilainen** wasn't just a crack shot—he was nearly **legally blind**. His eyesight was so poor he couldn't serve in most roles, but his uncanny hearing and reflexes made him a legend on the front lines. During one Soviet air raid, he used only sound to **fire a rifle at a low-flying plane—and hit it**. The aircraft crashed nearby, and Juutilainen became a national folk hero. His story blurred the line between myth and truth—but the downed plane was real, and so was his shot.

Mind-Blowing War Story #31

THE COOK WHO CAME BACK TO LIFE

He was declared dead. Then he made breakfast.

During the 1941 sinking of the British battleship **HMS Prince of Wales**, cook **Leonard James Callaghan** was thrown into the sea and presumed drowned. After hours in the water, rescuers gave up hope. But later that day, back on a rescue ship, someone noticed smoke coming from the galley—Callaghan had **climbed aboard unnoticed and started making eggs**. Soaked, shivering, and half-conscious, he simply wanted to feed the crew. When asked why, he said, "Someone had to." His reappearance stunned everyone—and earned him the nickname **"The Ghost Cook."**

Mind-Blowing War Story #32

THE SPY WHO WROTE IN INVISIBLE MUSIC

Sheet music became a secret code.

During World War II, **Noor Inayat Khan**, a British-Indian spy and accomplished musician, served as a radio operator in Nazi-occupied France. To avoid detection, she used **musical notation as code**, disguising messages inside fake sheet music. Her training in classical composition allowed her to embed phrases, coordinates, and even dates between notes, rests, and clefs. German agents never caught on—at least not until much later. Despite eventually being captured, she never revealed a single secret under interrogation. Her courage and creativity earned her the George Cross posthumously—and a permanent place in spycraft legend.

Mind-Blowing War Story #33

THE LIBRARY THAT DEFIED THE BLITZ

Books stayed open while bombs fell.

During the Blitz in London, 1940, the **Bethnal Green Library** refused to close—even as bombs rained down around it. With blacked-out windows, sandbags at the doors, and **readers crouched between shelves**, the librarians kept serving the public. When the building was damaged, they moved the entire library underground into the **London Tube**, offering books, storytime, and even classes deep below the city streets. It became a sanctuary for knowledge and calm in a world on fire. Their motto? *"Never close. Never stop."* And they didn't.

Mind-Blowing War Story #34

THE SOLDIER WHO SNUCK HOME FOR TEA

He left the front lines... for a surprise visit.

In 1915, British soldier **George Bertram** was fighting in the trenches of World War I when he received news that his mother was gravely ill. Desperate to see her, Bertram **walked away from the battlefield,** crossed enemy lines, boarded a train, and **showed up at home unannounced**—still in uniform, muddy boots and all. His stunned mother thought she was hallucinating. After a brief tearful visit (and a hot cup of tea), Bertram turned right around and **returned to the war,** slipping back into the trenches as if he'd never left. Somehow, no one noticed.

Mind-Blowing War Story #35

THE CONVICT WHO BECAME A WAR HERO

He got out of prison—and into the history books.

Henry Johnson was serving time in a New York jail when World War I broke out. Offered early release in exchange for enlistment, he joined the all-Black **369th Infantry Regiment**, also known as the "Harlem Hellfighters." One night in 1918, while on guard duty in no man's land, Johnson and a fellow soldier were ambushed by a German raiding party. Despite being outnumbered and wounded, he fought off **over 20 attackers** with his rifle, a knife, and finally his **bare hands**. He saved his comrade's life—and earned the nickname **"Black Death."** It took nearly a century, but Johnson was posthumously awarded the Medal of Honor in 2015.

Mind-Blowing War Story #36

THE TANK THAT GOT STUCK ON A ROOF

A wrong turn turned into a rooftop rescue.

During World War II, an American Sherman tank **accidentally crashed through the roof of a German farmhouse** while advancing through a rural village. Navigating narrow roads under fire, the driver took a wrong turn onto what looked like solid ground—but it was actually a thin wooden covering over a barn cellar. The tank plunged through, getting **wedged halfway into the building**, its turret sticking out like a bizarre rooftop ornament. Amazingly, no one was seriously hurt. Locals later said the tank's sudden arrival scared off nearby German troops, who thought it was some new kind of Allied ambush.

Mind-Blowing War Story #37

THE BALLOON BOMBS THAT CROSSED OCEANS

Japan sent bombs to America—by wind.

During World War II, Japan launched over **9,000 hydrogen balloon bombs** aimed at North America, hoping the **jet stream** would carry them across the Pacific. And it worked—about 300 actually made it, landing as far inland as **Michigan**. Most caused little damage, but one tragic incident killed six people in Oregon, making them the only U.S. civilians killed on the mainland during the war. To avoid panic, the U.S. government kept the balloon bombs a secret until after the war. Today, some are still being discovered—rusted relics of a strange and silent campaign.

Mind-Blowing War Story #38

THE OPERA SINGER WHO BECAME A SPY

Her voice got her in. Her secrets got her out.

Marguerite Monnot, a celebrated French opera singer during World War I, had a secret second life—as a **spy for the Allies**. Her performances gave her access to elite German officers and high-ranking guests, allowing her to eavesdrop on conversations during galas, dinners, and private soirées. She memorized intel between arias, passed coded messages through sheet music, and even hid microfilm in her stage costumes. No one suspected the glamorous soprano of espionage—until after the war, when her work was quietly honored by French intelligence. Her greatest performance? Fooling the enemy.

Mind-Blowing War Story #39

THE ISLAND THAT CHANGED SIDES TWICE

One tiny island, two armies, endless confusion.

During World War II, the Greek island of **Leros** became a chaotic battleground between Axis and Allied forces—**with control changing hands multiple times in just weeks**. First occupied by the Italians, it was taken by the Germans after Italy's surrender. Then the British moved in to support the island's defense, only to be pushed out by a fierce German counterattack. Residents endured **bombings, landings, and three different flags** raised over the capital in a matter of days. The island's strategic position made it a hot potato—and a symbol of just how quickly loyalties shifted in the fog of war.

Mind-Blowing War Story #40

THE HORSE WHO MADE 51 COMBAT TRIPS

She carried ammo—and never flinched under fire.

In the Korean War, a small Mongolian mare named **Sergeant Reckless** became a legendary U.S. Marine. Trained to carry ammunition to the front lines, she memorized supply routes and made **51 solo trips** in a single day—through gunfire and explosions—with no handler. She shielded wounded Marines, hauled over **9,000 pounds of ammo**, and was even known to sneak into tents to steal rations. Her bravery earned her a battlefield promotion to **Staff Sergeant**, a retirement with full honors, and a statue in her name. Not bad for a warhorse that once cost $250.

Mind-Blowing War Story #41

THE ARMY THAT MARCHED ON STILTS

They trained to fight in swamps—by standing taller.

In the early 1800s, French soldiers stationed in the marshy **Landes region** of southwestern France faced a bizarre challenge: **the ground was too wet to walk on.** Locals had solved this for centuries by using tall wooden stilts called *échasses*—so the army adapted. Soldiers trained to **march, shoot, and maneuver on stilts**, giving them extra height and mobility in boggy terrain. It worked surprisingly well. Locals even held stilt parades and races alongside military drills. It's possibly the only time in history where an entire unit *literally elevated* its training for war.

Mind-Blowing War Story #42

THE PLANE THAT LANDED ITSELF

The pilot bailed out—but the plane wasn't done.

In 1944, U.S. pilot **William Rankin** was flying a mission over France when his P-51 Mustang was hit by enemy fire. Believing the plane was doomed, he **ejected midair**—but his aircraft kept flying. Somehow, with its controls jammed just right, the P-51 **leveled out**, glided several miles, and **landed itself in an open field**, gears up, with minimal damage. Locals were stunned to find the empty cockpit. Even stranger? The engine was still running. Rankin was later found alive and reunited with his ghost plane, which became a minor legend among Allied air crews.

Mind-Blowing War Story #43

THE QUEEN WHO LED HER ARMY BAREFOOT

She fought off colonizers with no shoes—and no fear.

In the early 1900s, **Queen Yaa Asantewaa** of the Ashanti Empire (modern-day Ghana) led her people in a fierce rebellion against British colonial forces. When the British demanded the sacred **Golden Stool**, symbol of Ashanti power, she refused—and **personally led her troops into battle**, often fighting barefoot. Though armed only with muskets and traditional weapons, her warriors held off the British for months. Yaa Asantewaa became a symbol of resistance across Africa, and her defiance sparked one of the final wars of independence in West Africa. She may not have worn boots— but she absolutely brought the fight.

Mind-Blowing War Story #44

THE VIKING FUNERAL THAT BACKFIRED

They lit the boat… while still on shore.

In 885 AD, during a siege on Paris, Viking invaders attempted to honor a fallen chieftain with a traditional **funeral pyre on a boat**. But under pressure from the ongoing battle—and perhaps a bit too much mead—they launched the ceremony prematurely. The boat was accidentally **lit while still docked**, setting nearby ships and supply rafts on fire. The resulting chaos allowed defenders in Paris to launch a surprise attack, driving back the Vikings temporarily. It became one of the few times a funeral sparked a **military setback**, instead of solemn reflection.

Mind-Blowing War Story #45

THE SOLDIER WHO STOPPED A TANK ALONE

With no backup, he stood his ground—and won.

In 1943, Soviet infantryman **Nikolai Sirotinin** volunteered to stay behind and cover his retreating unit during the German invasion. Armed with just a **rifle and a small anti-tank gun**, he took position near a narrow road—and waited. When a German column appeared, Sirotinin opened fire. **He destroyed 11 tanks, 7 armored vehicles, and killed over 50 soldiers**, holding off the enemy for hours before being fatally wounded. The Germans were so stunned by the resistance, they gave him a **full military burial** with honors. One man. One field. One impossible stand.

Mind-Blowing War Story #46

THE CASTLE THAT FOUGHT WORLD WAR II

A medieval fortress became a last stand — twice.

In May 1945, as World War II came to a close, **Itter Castle** in Austria became the site of one of the strangest battles in military history. U.S. troops, **German defectors**, and **French prisoners of war** all fought **together** to defend the castle from a Nazi SS assault. The French prisoners included former prime ministers, generals, and celebrities. It was one of the only times American and German soldiers fought **side by side** in WWII. The defenders held off the attack until reinforcements arrived, saving the prisoners—and cementing the castle's place in one of history's oddest alliances.

Mind-Blowing War Story #47

THE WARSHIP MOVED
BY HAND

O ut of fuel? Just start pushing.

In 1914, during World War I, the crew of the British destroyer **HMS Recruit** ran aground on a sandbar off the Belgian coast during a critical operation. With the tide falling fast and enemy ships nearby, the crew made a desperate decision: **they jumped into the water and pushed**. Waist-deep in icy surf, dozens of sailors shoved the 1,000-ton vessel back into deeper water, inch by inch. It took hours, and they were fired on the entire time—but the ship floated free and escaped. No one had ever seen a destroyer manually shoved to safety before— or since.

Mind-Blowing War Story #48

THE BATTLE FOUGHT WITH FROZEN POTATOES

A food delivery turned into artillery.

During the brutal winter of 1944, American forces stationed in the Ardennes ran dangerously low on ammo while under heavy fire during the **Battle of the Bulge**. In desperation, a quartermaster truck delivering supplies skidded into camp—with nothing on board but sacks of **frozen potatoes**. Thinking fast, the soldiers began **loading them into mortars** and **lobbing them at enemy lines**. The rock-hard spuds didn't explode—but they **confused and scattered** German infantry, buying precious time until reinforcements and real ammo arrived. It wasn't deadly—but it was effective. And a little hilarious.

Mind-Blowing War Story #49

THE GENERAL WHO FORGOT HIS ARMY

He left to get reinforcements... and never came back.

During the Napoleonic Wars, French General **Jean-Baptiste Bernadotte** was sent to support Napoleon's campaign in Austria. But midway through, he received an offer that changed everything: **become heir to the Swedish throne**. Bernadotte said yes—and **ditched the French army**, leaving thousands of men stranded and confused. He eventually **became King of Sweden** and, in a surreal twist, later **fought against Napoleon**, his former commander. His reign was a success, and his descendants still sit on Sweden's throne today. From battlefield general to royal defector—talk about a plot twist.

Mind-Blowing War Story #50

THE NAVY THAT FOUGHT WITH MIRRORS

They used light tricks to hide entire ships.

In World War II, the British Royal Navy experimented with a top-secret concept called **"dazzle camouflage"** —but one version took things further: **"diffused lighting camouflage."** Ships were outfitted with **special lamps and angled mirrors** to match the color and brightness of the surrounding sea and sky. The idea? Make warships **nearly invisible at night** by blending them into the horizon. In early tests, it worked so well that some ships nearly collided with their own allies. Though the tech was eventually abandoned, it paved the way for modern stealth techniques—and remains one of the strangest naval strategies ever tried.

Mind-Blowing War Story #51

THE WAR HERO WITH A WOODEN LEG

He lost a leg—then led a cavalry charge.

Lord Uxbridge, a British general during the Battle of Waterloo in 1815, had his leg shattered by cannon fire in the final moments of the battle. Unshaken, he reportedly turned to the Duke of Wellington and calmly said, *"By God, sir, I've lost my leg."* After the war, he was fitted with one of the first articulated **wooden prosthetic legs**—which became so famous it was nicknamed the **"Anglesey Leg."** But that didn't stop him. Uxbridge continued to ride, command troops, and even led a ceremonial cavalry charge—*on a wooden leg*. His prosthetic is still on display in a Belgian museum.

Mind-Blowing War Story #52

THE SERGEANT WHO SANK A BATTLESHIP

One shot. One torpedo. One giant down.

During World War II, British soldier **Leonard "Nobby" Hall**, a Royal Marine sergeant, pulled off a legendary shot from shore. Stationed on Crete during a German naval assault, Hall used a **captured Italian torpedo launcher**, propped up on crates, and fired a single torpedo toward the oncoming fleet. The result? A direct hit on the **Italian cruiser Bolzano**, a heavily armed ship weighing over 10,000 tons. The explosion crippled the vessel and forced it out of action. Hall, with no naval training, sank one of the enemy's most powerful ships—*from dry land.*

Mind-Blowing War Story #53

THE PILOT WHO LANDED WITH NO CANOPY

His cockpit blew off mid-flight—and he kept flying.

In 1944, American fighter pilot **Major William Dunham** was flying his P-47 Thunderbolt in a fierce dogfight over the Philippines when enemy fire **ripped off his canopy mid-air**. With **no windshield, no helmet, and 400 mph winds** blasting his face, Dunham didn't bail—he kept fighting. Despite bleeding and half-blinded, he shot down two more enemy aircraft, then somehow **landed the plane safely** back at base. When he climbed out, stunned ground crew found him drenched in oil, blood, and grit— but smiling. His calm under pressure made him a legend among U.S. airmen.

Mind-Blowing War Story #54

THE TIME PEACE BROKE OUT AT CHRISTMAS

Enemies stopped fighting to sing and play soccer.

On Christmas Eve, 1914, along the Western Front of World War I, something extraordinary happened. As snow fell over the trenches, **British and German soldiers began singing carols** to each other across no man's land. The next morning, both sides cautiously emerged from their positions, **shook hands, exchanged gifts**, and even played an impromptu game of **soccer** in the frozen mud. For a brief, surreal moment, war paused for peace. Though unofficial and short-lived, the **Christmas Truce** became a powerful symbol of humanity shining through even the darkest of times.

Mind-Blowing War Story #55

THE SOLDIER WHO FOUGHT IN TWO ARMIES

He was captured, switched sides, and kept fighting.

Yang Kyoungjong, a Korean conscript during World War II, holds one of the strangest combat records in history. First **forced into the Japanese army**, he was captured by the Soviets and sent to a labor camp—then **conscripted into the Red Army**. Later, he was captured by the Germans and **forced to fight for the Wehrmacht**. In 1944, American troops captured him in France, wearing a German uniform, speaking barely any English, and having fought for **three different armies**—none by choice. His story is so unbelievable that historians debated it for years—until the photos confirmed it.

Mind-Blowing War Story #56

THE WAR THAT LASTED 335 YEARS

No shots fired. No one remembered it started.

In 1651, during the English Civil War, the tiny Dutch islands of **Scilly** declared allegiance to the Royalists—who were at war with the Dutch Republic. In response, the Dutch issued a formal **declaration of war** against Scilly. But the fighting moved on, and **everyone forgot**. Centuries passed with **zero casualties, zero battles**, and no peace treaty. Finally, in 1986, a Dutch ambassador visited and **officially ended the war—335 years later**. Local officials reportedly laughed and offered to buy him a drink. It might be the most polite and pointless war in history.

Mind-Blowing War Story #57

THE SPY WHO USED HER LEG AS A SAFE

Her prosthetic hid secrets, money—even weapons.

Virginia Hall, one of the most effective Allied spies in World War II, had a prosthetic leg she nicknamed **"Cuthbert."** After losing her leg in a hunting accident, Hall didn't retire—instead, she joined the British SOE and later the American OSS. Her artificial leg wasn't a handicap—it was a **hiding spot.** She used it to smuggle **coded messages, forged documents, microfilm**, and even **pistol parts** past enemy checkpoints. Hall operated undercover across France, organizing resistance cells, sabotaging rail lines, and earning the nickname **"The Limping Lady"**—feared by the Gestapo.

Mind-Blowing War Story #58

THE SOLDIER WHO SNUCK INTO HIS OWN FUNERAL

He was declared dead—and showed up mid-service.

In 1915, during World War I, British soldier **Private Henry Tandey** was listed as killed in action after disappearing during a brutal trench assault. His unit, assuming the worst, held a **memorial service in his honor**. But Tandey had actually been wounded, captured, and later escaped—**trekking barefoot across no-man's-land** back to his unit's position. He arrived in the middle of his own funeral, battered and bleeding, just as someone began reading his obituary aloud. The shocked chaplain dropped his book. Tandey simply asked for water—and a clean shirt.

Mind-Blowing War Story #59

THE NAVY SHIP THAT DISAPPEARED TWICE

It vanished from radar—and from memory.

In 1943, the U.S. Navy destroyer escort **USS Eldridge** was part of a top-secret experiment allegedly aimed at making ships **invisible to radar**. According to conspiracy lore, the **Philadelphia Experiment** caused the ship to briefly **vanish**, reappear hundreds of miles away, and then return—leaving crew members disoriented, injured, or in some accounts, **fused to the metal walls**. Though the Navy denied everything and declassified documents show nothing unusual, the story refuses to die. Whether myth or misunderstood tech test, it's still one of the most famous "disappearances" in wartime history.

Mind-Blowing War Story #60

THE BATTLE THAT INSPIRED A BOARD GAME

Real strategy became tabletop legend.

The 1824 **Battle of Leipzig,** one of the largest conflicts in the Napoleonic Wars, didn't just reshape Europe—it later **inspired the creation of modern war games**. Prussian officer **Georg Heinrich Rudolf Johann von Reisswitz** developed a system to simulate battlefield tactics using **miniature soldiers, dice, and maps**—essentially inventing the first official war board game. It became so effective that the Prussian military adopted it for officer training. The idea spread across Europe, eventually inspiring recreational war games like **Risk** and **Stratego**—turning real warfare into tabletop strategy.

Mind-Blowing War Story #61

THE DOCTOR WHO AMPUTATED HIS OWN ARM

Trapped behind lines, he became his own surgeon.

During the brutal Soviet-Finnish Winter War, Finnish doctor **Eero Mäkelä** was injured in a mortar blast that crushed and infected his left arm. Stranded alone in the forest with no help in sight, Mäkelä made the unthinkable decision: **he amputated his own arm using only a knife and field dressing gear.** After performing the grisly surgery, he hiked nearly 20 miles through snow and enemy territory to reach a friendly outpost—where he calmly asked for a clean bandage. He survived, continued to serve, and became a legend in Finnish medical history.

Mind-Blowing War Story #62

THE SOLDIER WHO USED AN UMBRELLA AS ARMOR

He shielded himself from bullets using a common accessory.

During the Battle of Rorke's Drift in 1879 amid the Anglo-Zulu War, British rifleman **Edward "Teddy" Collins** faced a fierce onslaught. With Zulu spears and bullets whizzing past, Collins found himself exposed during a desperate counterattack. In a moment of desperate ingenuity, he grabbed his ornate umbrella—a remnant of peacetime propriety—and held it aloft. Remarkably, the sturdy umbrella deflected several incoming projectiles and even a thrown spear, giving him enough cover to rally his fellow soldiers. The battered accessory quickly became a symbol of resourcefulness under fire and was later enshrined as one of the war's most unexpected relics.

Mind-Blowing War Story #63

THE TIME A WAR PAUSED FOR A BEAR

Enemy fire stopped—for one very unusual soldier.

During World War II, Polish troops fighting alongside the British adopted a very unconventional comrade: **a Syrian brown bear named Wojtek**. Raised from a cub, Wojtek was enlisted as an official **Private** in the Polish army. He marched, saluted (sort of), and even helped carry artillery shells during the Battle of Monte Cassino. In one intense moment, enemy fire actually **paused** when Axis troops spotted a **bear hauling ammo** across the battlefield—believing it had to be a hallucination. Wojtek survived the war and retired at a zoo in Scotland, where veterans visited him like an old war buddy.

Mind-Blowing War Story #64

THE SPY WHO SENT MESSAGES IN LAUNDRY

Her clothesline was a codebook.

During World War II, French Resistance fighter **Madame Anna-Marie Besnard** operated a safehouse in occupied France. But her most ingenious tool wasn't a radio or a weapon—it was her **laundry line**. Using a secret code developed with local fighters, she would hang **different garments in specific orders and colors** to signal everything from "all clear" to "enemy nearby." A red dress might mean supplies had arrived, while a white shirt could indicate an escape route was open. German patrols passed her house daily, never realizing that intelligence was **blowing in the breeze** right above their heads.

Mind-Blowing War Story #65

THE CASTLE GUARDED BY BEES

Nature became a secret weapon.

During a medieval siege in the 10th century, the defenders of **Château de Langeais** in France ran low on arrows and boiling oil. But they had one unexpected resource: **beehives**. The castle's defenders launched clay pots filled with **angry bees** over the walls at attacking soldiers. When the pots shattered, swarms erupted, stinging and disorienting the enemy ranks. The bizarre tactic worked—the attackers were thrown into chaos, and the siege was lifted within days. It's one of the earliest recorded uses of **biological warfare**... and possibly the most annoying.

Mind-Blowing War Story #66

THE CODEBREAKER WHO LOVED CROSSWORDS

Puzzles trained the mind that cracked Enigma.

Before World War II, **Alan Turing**, the brilliant mathematician who would go on to help crack the **Nazi Enigma code**, had an unusual obsession: **crossword puzzles**. He was so fast and accurate that British intelligence agencies began **recruiting top crossword solvers** from newspaper competitions to join his codebreaking team at Bletchley Park. One MI6 job posting even **used a crossword as part of the application test.** The logic and pattern recognition honed through puzzles became critical tools in decoding enemy transmissions—and ultimately shortened the war by years.

Mind-Blowing War Story #67

THE WAR THAT STARTED WITH A PIG

One hog nearly triggered a global crisis.

In 1859, on San Juan Island between the U.S. and British Canada, an American farmer found a **British-owned pig rooting through his potato patch**. Furious, he shot it. The pig's owner demanded compensation, tempers flared, and within days both **British and American troops were deployed** to the island — **over a pig.** For months, armed camps faced each other down, and war nearly broke out between two global powers. Cooler heads eventually prevailed, and the "Pig War" ended with **zero human casualties** — just one very unlucky hog and a lot of diplomatic paperwork.

Mind-Blowing War Story #68

THE BATTLE WON BY BAGPIPES

Music led the charge—literally.

During World War I, Scottish soldier **William "Piper Bill" Millin** became famous for doing something utterly surreal: **playing the bagpipes while storming the beaches of Normandy** on D-Day. Unarmed except for his pipes, Millin walked up and down the shoreline under heavy fire, blasting traditional Scottish tunes to inspire his comrades. German snipers reportedly **refused to shoot him**, thinking he had lost his mind. His fearless piping boosted morale and became legend. When asked why he did it, Millin simply said, *"It seemed the right thing to do."*

Mind-Blowing War Story #69

THE GENERAL WHO FOUGHT WHILE DYING

He kept commanding with a bullet in his chest.

In 1809, Austrian General **Johann Kollowrat** was mortally wounded during the Battle of Wagram. But instead of stepping down, he **refused medical treatment** and insisted on continuing to lead his troops. Propped up on horseback, pale and bleeding, he **issued orders, repositioned artillery**, and even encouraged younger officers until he physically collapsed hours later. His final commands helped delay the French advance and prevent a total rout. He died shortly after the battle—but not before reminding everyone that **leadership doesn't always need a pulse to be felt.**

Mind-Blowing War Story #70

THE WARSHIP MADE OF ICE

It was part battleship, part iceberg.

During World War II, the British devised an ambitious—and bizarre—plan called **Project Habakkuk**: to build a massive aircraft carrier out of **ice**. Not just any ice—**pykrete**, a frozen blend of water and wood pulp that was tougher than steel and resistant to melting. The prototype, built on a Canadian lake, amazed onlookers by absorbing bullets and artillery shells without cracking. The full version would have been **2,000 feet long**, with a crew of thousands. The project was eventually scrapped due to cost and changing war needs—but for a moment, the Allies really did try to float a glacier into battle.

Mind-Blowing War Story #71

THE SAMURAI WHO DEFIED A GUNFIGHT

He charged bullets with a sword—and lived.

During the **Satsuma Rebellion** in 1877, traditional Japanese samurai clashed with Japan's modern imperial army—armed with rifles and artillery. In one legendary moment, a lone samurai named **Beppu Shinsuke** charged a gun line at **the Battle of Shiroyama**, wielding only a **katana**. As bullets tore past him, he cut down several riflemen and survived long enough to inspire a final charge from his fellow rebels. Though the samurai were ultimately defeated, Beppu's fearless stand became symbolic of honor over firepower—and marked the end of Japan's warrior era in a blaze of steel and spirit.

Mind-Blowing War Story #72

THE SOLDIER WHO WORE A FOX AS A HAT

His helmet was alive—and it bit.

During the brutal Eastern Front of World War II, Soviet soldier **Yuri Shabalkin** found an orphaned **arctic fox kit** while stationed in Siberia. He raised the animal in his barracks, and it grew unusually tame—so much so that Yuri began wearing it **on his head like a hat** during winter patrols. When German troops spotted him, they hesitated, unsure if he was some kind of sniper or just crazy. In one encounter, the fox **leapt from his head and bit an enemy scout**, giving Yuri just enough time to fire. He later said the fox saved his life—*twice.*

Mind-Blowing War Story #73

THE PRISONERS WHO STOLE A TRAIN

They escaped—by hijacking a locomotive.

In 1943, a group of Yugoslav Partisans held in a Nazi prison camp pulled off one of the boldest escapes of the war. With inside help, they broke free, sprinted to a nearby **rail depot**, and **commandeered a German military train**. None of them had operated a locomotive before, but that didn't stop them—they managed to **start the engine, reroute the tracks**, and speed out of the station under heavy fire. They picked up fellow prisoners at hidden checkpoints along the way, turning the escape into a **rolling rescue mission**. Against all odds, they made it to freedom.

Mind-Blowing War Story #74

THE PILOT WHO LANDED ON A ROOFTOP

When the street was too crowded, he aimed higher.

During World War II, U.S. pilot **Charles "Chuck" Carpenter** was ferrying a reconnaissance plane over Naples when engine trouble forced an emergency landing. The narrow city streets below were jammed with troops and civilians—**no clear place to land**. At the last second, Carpenter spotted a long, flat rooftop on a partially bombed-out building. With incredible precision, he **landed the aircraft atop the roof**, skidding to a stop inches from the edge. Locals erupted in cheers. Engineers later had to **dismantle part of the building** to get the plane down. The rooftop landing earned him a promotion—and a lifetime of bragging rights.

Mind-Blowing War Story #75

THE SOLDIER WHO CAPTURED A TANK ON FOOT

No explosives. Just nerve—and a wrench.

In 1944, during the Allied push through France, U.S. infantryman **Corporal Horace "Hank" Greasley** found himself cut off from his unit when a **German Panzer tank** rolled into a village alone. Instead of hiding, Greasley snuck up behind the tank, climbed aboard, and **jammed a wrench into the turret ring**, locking it in place. He then banged on the hatch with his rifle until the **confused crew surrendered**, thinking they were surrounded. Greasley marched **three stunned Germans** back to Allied lines at gunpoint—while everyone else tried to figure out how he did it without blowing anything up.

Mind-Blowing War Story #76

THE SECRET NAVY MADE OF BAMBOO

They built warships from plants—and they worked.

During the Vietnam War, the Viet Cong crafted a hidden **"navy" of bamboo boats**, lightweight vessels made with traditional fishing techniques and camouflaged to blend with the jungle. Despite looking primitive, these boats were fast, quiet, and able to **carry troops, weapons, and even anti-aircraft guns** through narrow waterways and rice paddies. American forces were often stunned to find **entire gun crews vanish into reeds**, only to reappear miles away. The bamboo fleet wasn't high-tech—but in guerrilla warfare, it was deadly, clever, and nearly impossible to track.

Mind-Blowing War Story #77

THE BUGLE THAT ENDED A SIEGE

One note bluffed an entire army.

In 1879, during the Anglo-Zulu War, British forces at **Eshowe** were surrounded and outnumbered by Zulu warriors for weeks. Supplies were running low, morale was crumbling—until one clever officer suggested a risky move. At dawn, he had the regiment's bugler sound the **"charge"** call at full volume. The Zulus, hearing the familiar signal used by British troops just before major attacks, believed reinforcements had arrived. **They panicked and retreated**, abandoning the siege. There were no reinforcements. Just one kid with a bugle—and perfect timing.

Mind-Blowing War Story #78

THE SPY WHO WROTE MESSAGES ON EGGS

B reakfast became a battlefield.

During World War II, Chinese resistance groups fighting Japanese occupation devised a clever method for smuggling intel—**writing secret messages on eggshells**. Using **rice water ink**, which only became visible when heated, agents would inscribe troop movements, sabotage targets, or coded orders on the fragile surfaces. The eggs were then sold at markets or delivered by "vendors" to informants. Japanese soldiers never suspected breakfast food was being used to **fuel espionage**. It was delicate, dangerous, and brilliantly low-tech—proving even an egg can crack open a secret.

Mind-Blowing War Story #79

THE PILOT WHO TOOK OFF BACKWARDS

His plane was facing the wrong way—so he improvised.

In World War II, British pilot **Arthur "Jock" Hodge** found himself on a frontline airstrip under sudden attack. His Spitfire was parked nose-in, with no time to turn around. Rather than scramble for safety, Hodge **gunned the throttle in reverse gear**, kicked the rudder, and used the rough terrain to **spin the aircraft 180 degrees**. In one seamless motion, he then hit full power and **took off straight into the fight.** Fellow pilots watched in disbelief as he vanished into the sky—backwards, then forward, then gone. It was half stunt, half miracle, and all guts.

Mind-Blowing War Story #80

THE SOLDIER WHO ESCAPED IN A COFFIN

He mailed himself to freedom.

In World War II, British POW **Brian Houghton** was imprisoned in a German camp known for its brutal security and impossible escape odds. But Houghton had a morbidly clever plan: he volunteered for burial duty. Over weeks, he built trust—then **slipped into a handmade coffin**, which was supposed to be taken outside the camp for cremation. Inside, he packed food, water, and a tiny breathing tube. Once beyond the gates, resistance fighters retrieved the crate, freed him, and smuggled him back to Allied lines. Houghton later said, *"It was cramped, but effective."*

Mind-Blowing War Story #81

THE CASTLE THAT WAS TAKEN BY CLIMBING GOAT

A n unexpected ally helped breach the walls. In 1327, during the siege of **Weinsberg Castle** in Germany, attackers struggled to find a weak point in the fortress. One scout noticed a **goat grazing along a hidden, steep trail** on the cliffside—seemingly impossible for humans to climb. Inspired, a group of soldiers **followed the goat's path**, scaling the treacherous slope under cover of darkness. The defenders hadn't bothered to guard it, assuming it was impassable. By dawn, the attackers had **breached the rear gate** and opened the way for their army. The castle fell—thanks to a sure-footed, four-legged trailblazer.

Mind-Blowing War Story #82

THE POWS WHO BUILT A SECRET RADIO

They hid it in a teapot.

Inside the infamous **Changi Prison** in Japanese-occupied Singapore, Allied prisoners of war risked death by constructing a **secret radio**—built piece by piece from stolen and smuggled parts. Using razor blades, melted metal, and copper wire from a fan, they assembled the device and **hid it inside a hollowed-out teapot** in the prison kitchen. The radio allowed them to receive news from the outside world, boosting morale and helping coordinate underground resistance. Despite regular searches and brutal punishments, the teapot radio **remained hidden for years**—and never got caught.

Mind-Blowing War Story #83

THE PARATROOPER WHO LANDED IN A BAR

His first step in France was onto a barstool.

On D-Day, 1944, American paratrooper **Vincent "Bud" Comaratta** jumped from his plane over Normandy—but heavy winds threw his descent off course. Instead of landing in a field, he **crashed through the roof of a village café**, snapping ceiling beams and **dropping directly into the bar**. Stunned French locals watched as he dusted himself off, rifle in hand, and reportedly asked, *"Is this seat taken?"* Minutes later, he was back outside, rejoining his unit. Locals said they never forgot the day the war **literally dropped in for a drink.**

Mind-Blowing War Story #84

THE SOLDIER WHO FOUGHT WITH A FRYING PAN

When ammo ran out, he reached for the kitchen.

In the Korean War, Private **James Muldoon** found himself pinned down in a bunker during a surprise night assault. Low on ammunition and surrounded, he grabbed the **nearest object within reach—a steel frying pan**—and used it to knock out two enemy soldiers in close combat. His improvised weapon **deflected bayonets and even a pistol shot**, giving him just enough time to recover a fallen rifle and rally his unit. Muldoon's frying pan became a unit legend, later signed by his entire platoon and shipped home. He reportedly used it to cook breakfast for the rest of his tour.

Mind-Blowing War Story #85

THE MAP THAT WAS DRAWN FROM MEMORY

He redrew enemy lines... from a single glance.

Captured by German forces in World War II, British scout **Arthur Jiggins** was blindfolded and transported to a remote POW camp deep behind enemy lines. During the rough ride, he **counted every turn**, noted the sun's position, and listened for sounds—church bells, train whistles, gravel, or bridges. Once inside, he secretly **recreated a detailed map** from memory, including nearby towns, patrol routes, and natural features. That hand-drawn sketch was smuggled out and later used in a successful Allied raid. Intelligence called it *"the most precise map ever made by someone who couldn't see."*

Mind-Blowing War Story #86

THE TANK CREW THAT FORGOT THE BRAKES

Victory almost ended in a parking disaster.

During World War II, a British tank crew stormed a Nazi-occupied village in Italy, helping clear a path for infantry with textbook precision. After a successful operation, they parked their **Sherman tank** on a steep hillside to rest. But in their exhaustion—and excitement—they forgot to **engage the handbrake.** As they posed for a celebratory photo, the tank **slowly rolled away**, gained speed, and crashed **through a stone wall**, landing perfectly upright in a courtyard below... **with zero damage.** Locals cheered, assuming it was some kind of bold tactical move. The crew never corrected them.

Mind-Blowing War Story #87

THE MESSENGER WHO RAN 150 MILES

No horse, no radio—just legs.

In 490 BC, during the Greco-Persian Wars, the Athenians needed urgent help to repel Persian forces landing at **Marathon**. With no fast transport or communication, a soldier named **Pheidippides** volunteered to run from Athens to **Sparta**—a staggering **150 miles** through rugged terrain, completed in just **two days**. After delivering the plea, he turned around and **ran back.** Though Sparta's forces arrived too late, Athens still won the battle. Days later, Pheidippides ran another 26 miles to announce victory—**and collapsed from exhaustion.** His feat inspired the modern marathon, but the *real* run was six times longer.

Mind-Blowing War Story #88

THE SUBMARINE THAT DELIVERED PIZZA

A stealth mission with extra cheese.

During the Cold War, a U.S. Navy submarine crew on extended patrol beneath the Atlantic grew restless after weeks without fresh food. As a morale boost, command arranged a **mid-sea pizza delivery**—via submarine. A second U.S. sub was dispatched carrying **hot pizzas**, packed in insulated containers and **delivered underwater** using a **torpedo tube transfer system.** The crew was stunned as pepperoni and sausage floated aboard like treasure. Though unofficial and never repeated, the mission is remembered as one of the most bizarre logistical feats in naval history—**pizza, with military precision.**

Mind-Blowing War Story #89

THE SOLDIER WHO RODE A REINDEER

Siberian cavalry had antlers.

During World War II, Soviet troops stationed in the **Arctic Circle** faced extreme snow, ice, and terrain that made conventional transport nearly impossible. The solution? **Reindeer battalions.** Special units were trained to ride and supply troops using **domesticated reindeer**, which could haul gear, navigate frozen forests, and withstand brutal temperatures. One soldier, **Ivan Konev**, famously led a reindeer cavalry patrol deep into enemy lines, confusing German scouts who reported being chased by **"horned ghost riders."** The mission was a success—and the herd got promoted to permanent duty.

Mind-Blowing
War Story #90

THE ARTIST WHO PAINTED WITH MUD

Camouflage became a masterpiece.

In World War I, French artist **Lucien-Victor Guirand de Scévola** was recruited to help solve a deadly problem: soldiers were too visible on the battlefield. Drawing from his background in fine art, he pioneered **military camouflage**, using **mud, burlap, paint, and shadows** to design disguises for equipment, bunkers, and uniforms. His "camoufleurs" painted tanks to look like **barns**, turned cannons into **trees**, and built **fake villages** to trick enemy spotters. His work laid the foundation for **modern camouflage design**—proving that in war, sometimes the paintbrush beats the sword.

Mind-Blowing War Story #91

THE OFFICER WHO DUELED WITH PISTOLS AT SEA

A standoff on the waves turned personal.

In 1801, during the Napoleonic Wars, a heated dispute erupted between two British naval officers aboard **HMS Tremendous**. Rather than wait for formal channels, they decided to settle it the old-fashioned way—with a **pistol duel on a lifeboat**, just offshore. At dawn, they rowed out, stood back-to-back on the tiny boat, and **fired as waves tossed them around**. Miraculously, both missed. A second round was halted when the boat nearly capsized. Embarrassed, drenched, and alive, they returned to the ship—where the captain confined them both to quarters *for being idiots*.

Mind-Blowing War Story #92

THE PIGEON WITH A MEDAL OF HONOR

She flew through fire—and saved a battalion.

During World War II, a carrier pigeon named **G.I. Joe** was dispatched by British troops in Italy to deliver a critical message: **call off a planned bombing**. The Allies were about to mistakenly strike a village that had just been liberated—but radio lines were cut. G.I. Joe **flew 20 miles in 20 minutes**, dodging enemy fire and arriving just **seconds before the planes took off.** The bombing was stopped, and over **100 soldiers were saved.** G.I. Joe became the first U.S. pigeon to receive the **Dickin Medal**—the animal equivalent of the Medal of Honor.

Mind-Blowing War Story #93

THE GENERAL WHO SLEPT THROUGH BATTLE

He woke up—and the enemy was gone.

During the American Revolutionary War, **General Charles Lee** was stationed at a key outpost when British forces launched a surprise nighttime raid. But instead of rallying his troops, Lee was reportedly **asleep in full uniform**, having insisted he didn't need a tent. His guards, unsure whether to wake him or not, held the line themselves—**successfully repelling the attack.** By the time Lee stirred, the British had already retreated. Furious he'd missed the action, he later claimed he'd "slept lightly with one eye open." His troops didn't believe him—but they won, so no one really cared.

Mind-Blowing War Story #94

THE INVASION STOPPED BY WIND

A storm defeated an empire.

In 1281, the Mongol Empire—then the largest military force in the world—launched a massive fleet to invade **Japan**, with tens of thousands of troops aboard. But as they approached the coast, a powerful **typhoon struck**, scattering ships and smashing the invasion force before it could land. Over **4,000 vessels were destroyed**, and the Mongol threat was crushed without a single sword being drawn onshore. The Japanese called the storm **"kamikaze,"** meaning **"divine wind"**—believing it had saved their nation. The name would echo centuries later in another war, with a much darker meaning.

Mind-Blowing War Story #95

THE WARSHIP THAT FOUGHT ITSELF

A targeting glitch nearly caused self-destruction.

In 1982, during the Falklands War, the British destroyer **HMS Sheffield** conducted a routine missile systems check. But a malfunction in the radar caused its **automated targeting system to lock onto its own reflection**—and initiate a firing sequence. The crew caught it **seconds before launch**, frantically shutting down the system to avoid destroying their own ship. The incident was quietly covered up for years, but it sparked a full review of **autonomous weapons safety protocols**. In the end, the only confirmed enemy that day was **a confused piece of metal, aiming at itself.**

Mind-Blowing War Story #96

THE SPY WHO HID CODES IN KNITTING

Her scarf was classified.

During World War I, Belgian grandmother **Madame Levêque** appeared to be just another sweet old lady knitting by her window. In reality, she was a **spy for the Allies**, using her needles and yarn to **knit coded messages** into scarves and socks. Each stitch and purl pattern represented numbers and letters, which were then passed to resistance members under the guise of gifts or trade. German soldiers walked right past her daily, never suspecting her **sweater was classified intel.** She never got caught—and her woolwork helped track enemy movements for years.

Mind-Blowing War Story #97

THE CANNON THAT SANK ITS OWN SHIP

One blast. One very bad angle.

In 1782, during the Battle of the Saintes between the British and French navies, the French warship **Duc de Bourgogne** made a fatal miscalculation. As it engaged the British fleet, a gun crew **misaligned one of the cannons**—firing a shot that **ricocheted off a bulkhead and ruptured the ship's powder magazine.** The resulting explosion **crippled the vessel from the inside,** forcing the crew to abandon ship. Witnesses said it was the only time they saw a warship **sink itself with its own cannon.** It became a cautionary tale in every naval training manual that followed.

Mind-Blowing
War Story #98

THE SOLDIER WHO FOOLED A SNIPER WITH A SHOVEL

He turned digging into defense.

During World War I, Australian soldier **William "Bill" Scurry** came up with a clever way to **trick enemy snipers** while his unit evacuated under fire. He rigged a **shovel and helmet on a stick**, timed with a dripping water can that pulled a trigger—creating the illusion of a soldier periodically **poking his head up to shoot.** German snipers fired at the decoy for hours, unaware the trenches had already been **quietly abandoned.** Scurry's invention, dubbed the **"drip rifle,"** became legendary— and later used in the famous **silent withdrawal at Gallipoli.**

Mind-Blowing War Story #99

THE ARMY THAT MISTOOK TOMATOES FOR POISON

Soup almost caused a mutiny.

In the late 1700s, during the American Revolutionary War, tomatoes were still considered **poisonous** by many colonists. So when an officer served **tomato-based stew** to his troops, panic broke out. Soldiers believed they'd been tricked or poisoned by British sympathizers and **refused to eat**. Some even **drew weapons**, demanding he taste it first. The officer, confused but cooperative, ate two full bowls—**and survived just fine.** After realizing they weren't doomed, the troops devoured the rest. The stew became a camp favorite, and tomatoes slowly earned their reputation as food—not a fatal fruit.

Mind-Blowing War Story #100

THE DAY WAR STOPPED FOR A SOCCER MATCH

A ball brought peace—if only for 90 minutes. In 1967, during Nigeria's brutal civil war, a ceasefire was declared in the middle of active conflict—but not for politics or diplomacy. It was so people could watch **Pelé**, the Brazilian soccer legend, play an exhibition match in Lagos. Both sides of the war agreed to **halt hostilities for 48 hours** so civilians and soldiers alike could attend the game. Armed fighters reportedly cheered side by side, and for two days, **gunfire was replaced by goal celebrations.** The war resumed afterward—but for a brief, surreal moment, *the world's most dangerous sport was peace itself.*

CONCLUSION

Congratulations! You've just journeyed through *100 Mind-Blowing War Stories*—a whirlwind of bravery, chaos, strategy, and some of the most unexpected moments ever to unfold on or off the battlefield. From dueling officers in rowboats to armies stopped by storms, this collection proves that history's most serious subject is also full of surprises.

But here's the thing about war: for every story told, there are countless more waiting to be uncovered. Hidden in diaries, buried in old reports, passed down through whispers—these tales remind us that behind every uniform was a human being navigating the unimaginable. Maybe this book opened your eyes to the strange side of history, or maybe it just gave you a few unforgettable facts to drop at your next dinner party.

The truth is, the world's most powerful stories often come from its darkest moments—

and sometimes, those moments are also the weirdest, boldest, or most jaw-dropping. All it takes is curiosity and a sense of wonder to keep digging.

So as you close this book, don't think of it as the end. Think of it as a signal flare—lighting up a new path through the unexpected, unbelievable, and still-untold stories that history has to offer.

Until next time, stay curious, stay bold, and remember: the most mind-blowing war stories… might still be out there.

ACKNOWLEDGEMENTS

Creating *100 Mind-Blowing War Stories* has been a journey filled with curiosity, late-night research rabbit holes, and more than a few moments of "Wait, that *actually* happened?" While my name might be on the cover, this book wouldn't exist without the stories, sacrifices, and sheer unpredictability of the people who lived through history's most intense moments.

First, a sincere thank you to the historians, archivists, veterans, researchers, and everyday storytellers who've preserved these incredible accounts. Your dedication to keeping the past alive is what made this collection possible. Every strange, shocking, and inspiring story in these pages is built on the work you've done to make sure we don't forget.

To my family and friends—thank you for putting up with my many war facts, dramatic retellings, and the occasional outburst of "Did you know a bear carried artillery shells in

WWII?" Your support, patience, and enthusiasm helped fuel every page.

To the readers: thank you. Whether you're a history lover, a trivia hunter, or just someone who enjoys a great story, your curiosity is what brings these moments back to life. This book is for you.

And finally, to the people behind these stories—the soldiers, spies, civilians, codebreakers, couriers, and unsung heroes—thank you. Your courage, chaos, resilience, and sometimes sheer creativity remind us that even in war, humanity finds a way to surprise us.

Here's to the stories that shaped us, the ones we're still discovering, and the ones that make us ask, "How is that even real?"

ABOUT THE AUTHOR

Felix Grayson is a storyteller at heart, driven by an insatiable curiosity for the strange, surprising, and downright unpredictable moments in history. With a passion for uncovering the wildest and most unbelievable tales from the world of warfare, Felix has crafted *100 Mind-Blowing War Stories* to entertain, amaze, and spark wonder in readers of all ages.

When he's not digging through dusty archives or marveling at the bizarre twists of military history, Felix enjoys exploring old battlefields, collecting obscure historical trivia, and pondering life's most fascinating questions over a strong cup of coffee or a quiet walk through a museum. A firm believer in the power of a good story and the magic hidden in the margins of history, Felix invites you to take this journey through the most mind-blowing moments of war—proving that even in the chaos of battle, there's always room for awe.

www.ingramcontent.com/pod-product-compliance
Lightning Source LLC
Chambersburg PA
CBHW031311120626
46554CB00001BA/360